To my favorite
Stork - with

Hugs&kisses from your
Koala Bear xoxo

Smashed Potatoes

SMASHED POTATOES

A Kid's-Eye View of the Kitchen

Edited by Jane G. Martel

Houghton Mifflin Company Boston

A portion of this book has
previously appeared in *McCall's*.

A 10 9 8 7 6 5 4 3 2

Library of Congress Cataloging in Publication Data

Martel, Jane G
  Smashed potatoes; a kid's-eye view of the kitchen.

  SUMMARY: Gives children's versions of their favorite
dishes such as "Basketti," "A whole turkey," and
"Banilla cake."
  "A portion of this book has previously appeared in
McCall's."
  1. Cookery.   [1. Cookery]   I. Title.
TX652.M29   641.5   74-10947
ISBN 0-395-19775-9

Printed in the United States of America

To the children of the Francis J. Muraco
Elementary School who gave me
lots of love, lots of laughs,
lots of gray hairs, and these wonderful
recipes and drawings.

Smashed Potatoes

"41 sausages as big as your ear"

Skabbetti

41 sausages as big as your ear

41 meatballs not as big

41 orange potatoes or tomatoes

41 skabbetti

41 clean oil

First you decide what will it be tonight — sausages or meatballs?

When your father tells you which one, then you cook.

Mix the sauce in the blender so your elbows don't hurt.

When the skabbetti is done from the cooking in the broiler (2 degrees or maybe 3), get it in the silver pan with holes in it by your spoon with holes in it.

Then spread out the sauce.

It serves your whole family and all your father's friends.

"your father has to stay home for the day"

Basketti
with macaronis and noodles

1 whole pack of long sticks — get them the size
    you want them.
Orangey-red spicy stuff for topping (2 little kinds
    and 2 big kinds)
1 half of a quarter of water
Many purple onions with the paper off
Use red meat balls and the soapy kind of cheese
    that tastes a little bit rotten.

For the cooking get a stove, and pots, and bowls, and
spoons and gloves with pink flowers.
    Cook it all for quite a while.
    The only thing is — when you have it, your father has
to stay home for the day because he takes the basketti
out of the pan and squeezes out the water.
    Serves all 4 of us — but not Freddy.

"some people have milk to drink and some have Martinis"

Plain noodles
'cause they're my best

1 little triangle of butter this big
1 whole thing of noodles
An amount of salt
The same of pepper
Whatever else you need

Take the thing with high edges (not exactly a pan) and put 10 pounds of boiling water in it. Put the noodles in for I wouldn't guess how long. Your mother knows because she can tell time. One thing for sure — when you touch them they feel slippery-wet.

I suppose you could have other stuff with it if you want . . .

And some people have milk to drink and some have martinis.

"then throw it up in the air over your head"

Pizza

½ of white cheese
1 full thing of red gravy
A lot of dough

Get the dough into a circle about size 14. Then throw it up in the air over your head.

Cook the gravy for a couple of hours or minutes. Then put it on the dough with a cookin' spoon — and pat it all around.

Take your gold square thing that makes the cheese all crumble up.

Then put on the gravy and cook it for a real long time.

If you don't get it out on time, it gets kinda blackish, but you still have to eat it.

Have it in the summer with popsicles and wine.

"say a prayer and eat"

Corn beef stew

To make this, first you have to get in the wagon and drive downtown.

Then you buy:

    The tall French-Italian bread
    The butter
    The clove
    The paper towels

Then you get in the wagon and drive back home.

Then take everything out and put it away. Put the bag between the cat food — but fold it up.

Cook it in the stove in your pan. Look in the window all the time to see if it's done.

Then say a prayer and eat.

Serves for a pretty long time if there's only 3 people.

(Eat out in between.)

"get up when the alarm says"

A whole turkey

1 big bag full of a whole turkey
   (Get the kind with no feathers on
   not the kind the Pilgrims ate.)
A giant lump of stuffin'
1 squash pie
1 mint pie
1 little fancy dish of sour berries
1 big fancy dish of a vegetable mix
20 dishes of all different candies; chocolate balls,
   cherry balls, good'n plenties and peanuts

Get up when the alarm says to and get busy fast. Unfold the turkey and open up the holes. Push in the stuffin' for a couple hours. I think you get stuffin' from that Farm that makes it.

I know you have to pin the stuffin' to the turkey or I suppose it would get out. And get special pins or use big long nails.

Get the kitchen real hot, and from there on you just cook turkey. Sometimes you can call it a bird, but it's not.

Then you put the vegetables in the cooker — and first put one on top, and next put one on the bottom, and then one in the middle. That makes a vegetable mix. Put 2 red things of salt all in it and 2 red things of water also. Cook them to just ½ of warm.

Put candies all around the place and Linda will bring over the pies.

When the company comes put on your red apron.

"wait till your father comes home from the dump"

A black steak

A five dollar steak
2 boxes of some ready kind of gravy
2 boxes of cob on the corn
2 boxes of potatoes with a picture of potatoes on it
1 box of salad-bowl salad

Put the steak on a skinny pan. Get the fire-hot stove ready, and tell all the kids to get out of the kitchen.

Put the blue dishes on the table, and you are all set.

Now just wait till your father comes home from the dump.

Serve the family and even the neighbors (if they are your friends).

"now it's time to eat"

Hot dogs

1 package of hot dogs that has a lot in it

3 whole packages of spinach — so then we have 2 left
over for 2 more nights

1 whole package of hot dog buns (you can use bread
if you don't have any — it tastes just as good to
my mother but not to me)

1 bottle of ketchup — a big one

only ½ bottle of mustard — because of how it tastes

½ of salad — put it on the left side

Put the hot dogs on a greasy pan. Cook it until your
mother puts the silverware on.

Now it's time to eat, and have a piece of your aunt's
cake.

Note: Of course you know that you put dressing
on the salad.

"8° (my mother thinks)

or 10° (my father thinks)"

Steak and smashed potatoes and apple pie

For Steak:

> 1 pound of steak with red meat in it
> 5 potatoes or 10 pounds
> 10 inches of salt

For Gravy:

> A whole of flour
> 6 inches of water

For Pie:

> 10 inches of dough
> 3 apples
> 7 pounds of sugar

Put the steak in a flat pan and put in on the stove at 8° (my mother thinks) or 10° (my father thinks) and cook for 4 hours.

Cut up the potatoes and smash them up and cook them in a big pot for the same time.

Then put the dough in a flat silver thing and smash with a potato smasher and then put on some more dough. Put it in the oven at 9° for 5 minutes.

Put everything on the table and you could have company.

Serves 4

And if my sister doesn't eat her carrots, she can't have any pie.

"stoves really is dangerous — and you shouldn't go near one
  till you get married"

Chops

Some chops that are enough to fill up your pan
Fresh salt and pepper
Fresh flour
1 ball of salad lettuce
1 sponge cake with ice cream

Put the chops in the bag and shake them for 5 hours
— and the flour too.

Put them in a skillet pan on the biggest black circle on
the roof of your stove. Cook them for plenty of time.

Fringe up the lettuce in little heaps in all the bowls.

Go on the porch and bring the high chair and have
your supper everybody!

Note: But stoves really is dangerous — and you
shouldn't go near one till you get married.

"do it some other day"

Meat for a cookout

1 dishful of potato chips
1 dishful of fruits
A grill
12 charcoals
The same of hamburgs and rolls so they will fit, or
    you will have some left over

Before you start spray your spray can out back and
kill all the bugs — or you can wait till the bugs all go
away somewhere else.

Then you start to get ready and squirt the can of
Vaseline all around the charcoals. Stand pretty far back
and light it to a fire.

But you can't cook till it's time to eat and the fire is
gone out. You don't need the fire anyway because you
cook the meat by the black smoke.

If it rains, get the arrangement off of the picnic table
and go in the house.

Do it some other day — like if you go camping to the
Grand Canyon.

"after you ate enough, ask to be excused"

Plain fish

3 plates of plain fish
1 can of crispo
1 can of vanilla
Some meal that isn't oatmeal — like Maypo
I don't know any more things

I know a fisherman has to go in a boat all night to catch the fish on his fishin' pole. It sure is a hard job all right.

The fish has to cook in a dinner pan and get out 3 little jars of pepper. Do 8 shakes up and 11 shakes down. Then you flip them with your pancake thing for 11 flips.

If you have tuna fish, there is no cooking because you can eat it raw inside of a sandwich.

Lobsters are a kind of fish too, and the fisherman has to catch them in a big wooden box.

If the fish gets done, you go to the table and light the candles — but leave the lights on or you won't see how good it is.

After you ate enough, ask to be excused.

All of the fish live in the ocean, and they never come out. They can swim a hundred miles.

"cook them one at a time"

Peas

3 potatoes
2 big chickens (30 pounds)
1 roast beef
2 packages of corn
2 big pumpkins

Cook them one at a time.

"serves my sister named Debbie"

Baked beans

14 bean seeds
100 sauce
20 salt
13 potatoes

Put the beans and sauce and salt and potatoes in a fry pan. Put it in the oven at 14° for an hour.

Then make a salad with lettuce and a thing that is red and round like an orange with a green stem on it. You can put in another thing that is little and round and black with a hole in it. Put it all in a brown bowl with mayonnaise.

Serves my sister named Debbie and Nanna and Mother and Daddy.

Note: Now I know what those little round black things with a hole in the middle are called — they're called ollibs!

"all kinds of people can eat it.
You don't have to be Chinese"

Chinese food

6 bones

2 sauce

20 inches of Chinese rice

1 basket of chowmeins

1 basket of Kung foo yung

6 tan cookies with paper inside

Warm it all good and hot while you bake it by the stove. Put the sauce on the bones. When they get red they are through with the baking.

Put the baskets on the table, and the rice and the red bones.

Eat it for dinner and leave the rest for leftovers. Then it is time to open up the cookies and read them.

It makes a Chinese dinner for 3 people. But all kinds of people can eat it. You don't have to be Chinese.

"first you open the eggs with your mittens"

Scrambled eggs
on a flat dish

5 pounds of boiled bacon
2 pounds of eggs
3 pounds of ginger ale
1 fat
8 gallon of salt
4 pounds of pepper
Corn flakes
1 knife of butter
A fork, a spoon and a dish

First you open the eggs with your mittens. You only use the inside. Throw the rest in the sink.

Put the eggs in a 10 pound pan and cook the bacon in a plastic pan.

Get your pan real hot. If you get your pan hot first, you only have to cook for 2 minutes. But if the pan is not hot, you have to cook for 3 hours.

Get on the shelf and find the flat dish.

Eat it in the morning or in the afternoon. And you will sure need some orange juice after.

"eat in a jiffy and get going"

Muffin cup cakes

A round glass of Aunt Jemima
A round glass of bakery powder
Another round glass of sugar
A spoon of another sugar
Some egg out of 1 egg shell
1 box of fruit-berries

Get a little screen and shake everything on it till it falls in the bowl.

Then get it wet and kind of hit it around in the bowl for a little while.

Then put the paper cups in a pan that will hold them up.

Cook them in the oven as fast as you can because its almost time to go.

When they turn to bread, hurry up and get the jelly and the butter.

Eat in a jiffy and get going.

It makes 2 for each plate.

"because *remember* — the cake
is the same size as the pan"

Apple cake

10 pounds of white food coloring
1 gallon of lovely good cake frosting
2 gallons of sugar
2 and 3 gallons of milk
1 gallon again of water
1 nice apple cake from the store

Put them all together in a bowl. Mix it with a spoon on a long stick so you don't get your hands down in the dip. Stir it for a gallon long.

Pour it in a round pot, and put it on the right side of the stove — till the big hand is on the six.

Then take them out and put them all together and we'll have cake!

It makes the number of pieces for a party or for dessert — because *remember* — the cake is the same size as the pan.

Note: If you don't like the frosting — just scrape it off — and *no* fussing!

"it makes a whole breakfast to our family — except my mother. She eats Special K"

French toast

10 breads
1 pour of milk
1 dish of butter
A lot of pours of maple syrup

Have a bacon pan or an egg pan to cook in and a shovel thing. You put it in the pan with your fingers, but you have to get it out with the shovel.

First you plop the bread into the bowl of milk. But take it out pretty soon or it will leak all over and fall apart.

Cook the wet breads in the pan for as long as you stand there — and it gets to be French toast.

Then put it on 4 dishes with sausages on them — and all the pours of syrup.

It makes a whole breakfast to our family — except my mother. She eats Special K.

"put every single thing you have in a mother-size pan"

Banilla cake

1 cake stuff

2 eggs (But on "Sesame Street" they put 8 eggs in a
cake. I always watch "Love American Style" after
"Sesame Street.")

A drop of milk

7 of those little silver baseballs for on the top.

Put every single thing you have into a mother-size pan
— a little one wouldn't do.

Put it in the oven department of the stove. Make it as
hot as a coffee pot.

Pretty soon it will come popping right out!

Eat it when the news comes on.

"get a high person"

Devil food eggs

1 box of dark white eggs

1 jar of dark yellow devil food

3 dots of regular white salt

3 dots of black pepper

3 dots of red powder

1 faucet of extra hot water

Use a pot of a lot of silver on the top and a little gold under. Put a lot of eggs and water in it. Cook it on the outside because the outside is the stove and the inside is the oven.

Get a high person to know when to stop the stove. Little kids don't know yet.

Then set down and cool off for 3 minutes and little more. But it's not over yet.

You have to chop the eggs in half till you see two pieces. Fill up the dents with devil food and put them in the refrigerator.

Wait around.

When you want them to come out to eat, you can put the red dots on.

They will taste very good to your mouth.

"it makes me so delicious"

Tappy apples

A handful of round apples

A handful of candy frosting

A handful of sticks that you save out of your
fudgicles. (Get one stick for one apple, 2 sticks
for 2 apples — like you are matching.)

1 thumb and finger of sugar for 1 apple — like
matching again

Put the candy in a special double pan (but only my
mother knows its name). Let them get hot enough not
to put your finger in.

Boil the candy things till it gets juicy and covers up
the apples. Then make them stand up on little kitchen
papers.

I don't think we *have* to let them cool off, but we can
if we want to.

And we will have however many we made.

It makes me so delicious that I wish I could have one
now!

"all over the kitchen — P O W ! P O W ! P O W !"

Popcorn

37 of those hard little seed things
   that 'splode into popcorn
3 hot butters to trickle on
1 dish of salt to throw all over it

Put the popcorn seeds in the popcorn bowl and plug it in the plug hold — and get the toaster out of the way.

It takes about 10 hours to get going — but if you wait, you would see something funny. If your brother takes the lid off, popcorn go zinging all over the kitchen — POW! POW! POW!

Go wash both of your hands because you need to eat it with fingers.

If you want to save it, put it in a big plastic Baggie and put it under your bed till tomorrow.

You just keep eating till it's all gone.

"her name is Myrna and she is a R E A L popsicle-eater"

Popsicles for summer

1 whole can of any kind of drink except for beer
11 or 9 sticks maybe
regular frigerator silver things that turns ice
  into squares

T H A T   I S   A L L

Shake up the juice for some hours. Be sure to put the sticks in upside down, else you won't have no handles, and maybe you could never get the popsicles out.

Now it has to freeze good — or — oh boy! — when you open it, it will spill all over, and the floor gets all sticky, and bad ants come.

Usually it takes till lunch time, but not always.

It serves the brothers and the sisters and my grandma — her name is Myrna and she is a R E A L popsicle-eater!

Notes: 1. Eat them only one at a time.
          2. Always eat them outdoors.

"I would put it in a truck"

Ice cream

6 inches of cream
6 inches of milk

Put everything in a box. Put it in the freezer for one whole half a hour.

Then it starts turning into ice cream because that's how it's made.

Then you could eat it, but I wouldn't. I would put it in a truck, and bring it to a milk store, and I would sell it to all the people for real money.

"because we put onions in everything"

Lemon pie

10 cherries

4 cream

2 boxes of lemony sweet ice cream

10 coconuts

Put it in a bowl. Then mixer it up or spatula it up.
Get a pan like glass, and put in the onion crust because
we put onions in everything.

It goes for 10 hours in the oven and 10 hours in the
refrigerator.

It makes 10 slices.